# F·R·I·E·N·D·S

## THE TELEVISION SERIES

# THE ONE ABOUT YOU

**If we were on *Friends*, our episode would be called: "The One Where**

"

they're both not 💕 .

**When I say "unagi," you say**

brun idk .

**Have I ever told you that**

............................................................................

**brings out your smile?**

**You understand that staying awake while**

I rant to u @night

**is an important part of friendship.**

**You would walk a mile for me, especially if**

I had a hot guy 4 you.

**I can count on you to listen (even when I don't ask) because you**

have the same problems .
as me

**When we put our heads together, we can**

......................................................................... .

**Real party or fake party, you're always down to**

dance

**for a friend.**

You accept my ~~I~~ your fear of

birds

and ~~don't~~ help me by

laughing

.

**Your taste in salmon is rivaled only
by your taste in**

men
............................................................ .

# "OOH-OOH-OOH, YEAH!"

I know it's wrong, but you look really classy in

_fluffy socks_ .

**In an alternate reality, you would be**

happy

**and I would be**

also happy .

**Your cooking skills are the reason why**

I cook .

**You appreciate what it means to "pivot" when**

.......................................................................... .

**If we had a name for our "routine" it would be**

"Jules sucks" the disstrack .

**We've had some of our best talks at** *on*

facetime making fun
of people

SERVICE

**It's hard to believe we ever used to look so**

_ugly_ .

**If we had a canoe, you'd be my**

..............................................................................................

**and we'd paddle from**

..............................................................................................

**to**

.................................................................................. .

(iak this one)
weird

**No one could ever take your place in my**

heart♡

We can get through anything together with a

_phone_

or a giant poking device.

**I'd pick you to be on my team for**

*anything*

**any day.**

**It's like you have a sixth sense for knowing exactly when I feel**

_____ .

**If you could *be* any more stylish, you would be**

.......................................................... .

what does this even mean?

"NO, YOU!"

When I can't find the words, you know just what to

......... say ......................................... .

**You really know how to motivate me to**

do stuff

**by**

telling me .

**If we both liked the same person, we would settle it by**

we wouldnt .

**There's no monkey business in our friendship . . . except the time when**

you unadded me
in 7th grade

**You make me feel**

special/loved

**on my birthday.**

**You gave me my very first**

true friendship

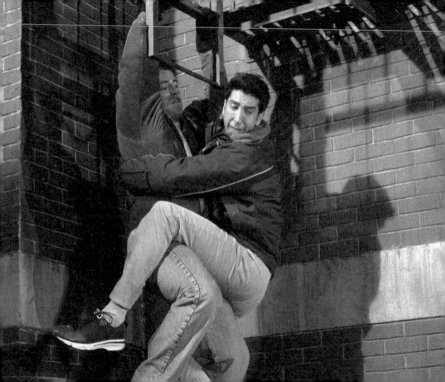

**"Face to face, or butt to face," you'd never leave me hanging on a**

_anything_ .

**If we had a friendship theme song, it would be**

the song that goes "& its always u & me, always & 4ever

~~sung by~~

from tik tok                                    .

I love that I never have to pretend to be

*anyone*

...................................................................................

with you.

**If we were super heroes, you would be**

spiderman

**and I would be**

I dk

**You really respect when I need some**

...................................................................................

time.

**You always make me feel better by**

making me laugh .

**Your**

........................................................................................

**talent is something that can
only be described as**

.................. *perfect* ......................................... .

**You're understanding when I'm
not having the best**

........................................................................

day.

**If we could travel anywhere together,
it would be to**

greece
....................................................................................................................... .

**If you change your name, promise me it will be something badass like**

_wnorahood_

**. . . or Princess Consuela Banana Hammock . . . or Crap Bag.**

# "HOW YOU DOIN'?"

**Our catch phrases include**

........................ good ........................

**and**

........................ perf ........................ .

**We have our own language that no
one understands except**

_____ us _____ .

# "WAY."
# "NO WAY."

**Our pact about**

we aont have a pact

**is the foundation of our friendship.**

**When we first met, we were bitchin'.
Now, we are**

_bitchin_ .

**You deserve a toast for being the best**

*friend*

ever.

**You know that I always have
your back, even when**

your sad

I'LL <u>ALWAYS</u> BE
THERE FOR YOU.

RP Studio
Hachette Book Group
1290 Avenue of the Americas, New York, NY 10104
www.runningpress.com
@Running_Press

Printed in China
First Edition: October 2019

Published by RP Studio, an imprint of Perseus Books, LLC, a subsidiary of Hachette Book Group, Inc. The RP Studio name and logo is a trademark of the Hachette Book Group.

The publisher is not responsible for websites (or their content) that are not owned by the publisher.

Text by Shoshana Stopek.
Design by Celeste Joyce.

ISBN: 978-0-7624-9609-9

1010

10  9  8  7  6  5  4  3  2